Save It! Keep It! Use It Again!

A Book About Conservation and Recycling

by R. J. LEFKOWITZ

illustrated by JOHN E. JOHNSON

A Finding-Out Book

Parents' Magazine Press • New York

for Iris,
who never said a word

Library of Congress Cataloging in Publication Data

Lefkowitz, R J 1942-
  Save it! Keep it! Use it again!

  (A Finding-out book)
  Includes index.
  SUMMARY: Discusses ways that scarce natural resources
can be conserved through recycling.
  1. Recycling (Waste, etc.)—Juvenile literature.
2. Conservation of natural resources—Juvenile literature. [1. Recycling (Waste) 2. Conservation of
natural resources]   I. Johnson, John Emil, 1929-
II. Title.
TD794.5.L43   333.7'2   76-27244
ISBN 0-8193-0896-X
10 9 8 7 6 5 4 3 2 1

What's In This Book

One
The Stuff of the Earth

The earth is full of stuff: sand and clay, cornstalks and hay, coal and oil, iron and soil. Then there are flowers and trees, birds and bees, dogs and cats, horses and bats. And lots more things.

People use most of the things found on the earth or underground.

We make glass out of sand, and statues of clay. Corn is good for eating, or for feeding to animals that we will eat later. Hay is also fed to animals on the farm, and it makes a good bed for them to sleep on besides.

Coal, oil, and other fuels found in the earth give us the energy to run our homes and factories and machines. We build things and even make our tools out of iron and other metals that we get from the earth. Farmers use the soil that covers the earth to grow the crops that we eat.

Perfumes and even medicines are made from flowers, and trees give us wood for making furniture and pencils.

Many birds eat insects that would otherwise eat the farmers' crops.

There are dogs that guard factories, and dogs that herd sheep, and dogs that help blind people

get around. And lots of dogs that people use for
pets, just as they do cats.

A horse can pull a wagon or help to plow a
field. Horses are also used to make food for dogs.

What on earth can you do with a bat?

Scientists study bats to find out how they can
fly in the dark. That helps us learn how to fly our
airplanes at night. And bats are also very useful
for making scary movies.

All of these things that we use are called *resources.* Because they are all found in nature, we call them *natural resources.*

The natural resources of the earth supply us with everything we need to live. Food, clothing, heat and light, living places, and anything else you can think of.

We depend on our natural resources for everything. They are all we have to work with.

Two

Resources That Live

A cow in the pasture is just as much a natural resource as a lump of coal in the mine. But there is one big difference between them: the cow is alive.

Many of the earth's resources are living things. That gives them one advantage over non-living resources. Living things can produce more of their own kind.

If you have some cattle on a farm, they can produce young cattle, just as dogs and frogs can produce new dogs and frogs. If you have some lumps of coal down in a mine, you will not get any new lumps of coal from them, no matter how long you wait.

Young cattle that grow up can replace older cattle that are killed for eating. Resources that can replace, or renew, themselves are called *renewable resources*. As new calves are born to replace older cattle that die or are killed, the supply of cattle is always being renewed.

The same is true for sheep and horses, and for other sorts of animals such as insects, fish, and birds.

Does this mean that we can never run out of a renewable resource? Unfortunately, it does not.

Suppose that each year a farmer killed more adult cattle than there were young ones born. Then the herd would get smaller each year. In time, there would be none left.

The same thing would be true if too many fish were fished out of a stream, or too many birds were shot out of the air.

Our animal resources can renew themselves year after year—if we are careful each year not to kill more than are born.

The plants that live and grow on the earth can also renew themselves time and time again. Trees, flowers, and grains and other grasses all have ways of producing young plants that will replace them when they die. But plants can also be used up too quickly to reproduce themselves in the numbers we need, when we need them.

Suppose a forester had 10 grown trees of a kind that took 10 years to grow to a usable size. If he cut them all down for lumber, then he would not have any more trees to use for another 10 years, even if he planted seeds immediately.

Instead of doing that, the forester could cut down just one tree each year. Then, by the time he got to cutting down the last fully grown tree, the first tree that he had planted would be ready for cutting the following year.

That could go on and on, year after year, tree after tree. If the forester were always careful to plant a new tree for each one he cut, and never to cut down too many at once, he could always have a good supply of trees and lumber.

So it is with crops and other plants, and with cattle, fish, birds, and other animals. If we are careful not to use too many at once, and if we make sure that there are enough young to replace the ones we use, then our living resources can renew themselves over and over again.

That is what conservation is all about. It doesn't mean not using our natural resources. It means using just some of those resources today, making sure that we will have some to use tomorrow.

Three

Resources That Die

Conserving our renewable resources is a good idea. But as with many good ideas, sometimes nobody listens to it.

In the United States there were once great flocks of a bird known as the passenger pigeon. It was a pretty bird to look at, and it made for some good eating, too. But you have never seen a passenger pigeon, much less tasted one. And you never will. There aren't any more.

When passenger pigeons were plentiful, no one thought that there would be a day when they weren't. So people ate them, and no one thought about raising young pigeons to replace the ones they ate. Until one day the pigeons were all gone—every last one.

Now some people might feel that was no great loss. After all, we do have other things to eat.

But many other people feel that when a particular kind of plant or animal dies out, we all lose something. Each kind of plant or animal is special in its own way. If it is gone, there will never be anything else quite like it.

Sometimes, too, losing one kind of plant or animal can cause us to lose another kind as well. If a certain kind of tree died out, what do you think would happen to birds that needed that kind of tree to live in?

There are many kinds of living things that are in danger of dying out, or becoming extinct. When a kind of plant or animal becomes extinct, it means there is not a single one left, and there will never be another.

And whenever that happens, our world seems to become a little bit poorer.

Conservationists—people who believe in conservation, and who practice it—try to keep the different kinds of plants and animals found on the earth from disappearing for good.

Sometimes that means passing laws to stop hunters from shooting a certain kind of

animal, or from shooting the young animals that
will replace the older ones. Sometimes it means
stopping builders from destroying forests or
marshes that a certain kind of animal or plant
needs to live in.

There are many laws to protect animals and
plants in danger of becoming extinct. Sometimes
people break those laws.

After a law was passed to protect alligators in
the United States, some people still hunted them.
They sold the alligator hides to people who made
wallets and purses and shoes out of them. Stores
bought the things made of alligator hide, and
sold them to people who wanted them.

Then it became against the law to sell anything made from an alligator. The stores stopped buying and selling the wallets, purses, and shoes. The people who made those things stopped buying the alligator hides. And many of the alligator hunters stopped hunting alligators, since they couldn't sell the hides any more.

That is one way to protect animals that are dying out. As more and more different kinds of animals and plants become fewer and fewer in number, we will find many new ways to protect them. Law makers will pass new laws, and scientists will learn new things that can help the living things that are in danger.

But the most important thing we will need is people who care whether some kind of animal or plant continues to live on the earth or is lost forever.

Do you care?

Four

Be Careful How You Use It

Even if all our living resources were to go on renewing themselves forever, we could still run out of some things that we need and use.

That is because many of the resources we depend on are not living things. And non-living things cannot renew themselves. Once we use them up, they are gone, and that's that. We cannot replace them.

Many of the raw materials that we use to

make things are non-renewable resources. Iron is one. We can make steel out of iron. But we can't make iron.

We can make brass out of copper and zinc. But we can't make copper or zinc. Glass can be made from sand and limestone. But first we have to have the sand and limestone.

Iron, copper, zinc, sand, and limestone are just a few of the raw materials we find in nature and cannot make ourselves. Sand is always being made as ocean waves wear down rocks on the shore, but that happens much too slowly for us to call sand a renewable resource.

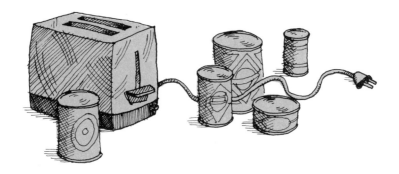

If a resource cannot renew itself, and if we cannot make it, then you would think that we have to be pretty careful about how we use it. And you would be right.

People have not always been very careful, though. A lot of metals have become less and less plentiful as we have used more and more of them to make more and more cars and cans and toasters. We are beginning to run out of some of the metals we use the most.

We are also getting close to running out of fuels such as gasoline and heating oil. We make gasoline and heating oil from petroleum. But we cannot make petroleum. It is true that we can make a kind of fuel oil out of coal. But then we cannot make coal.

If we were to run out of our metals and fuels, and our minerals, such as limestone, we would be in real trouble. We would not be able to build our factories, cars, and air conditioners, or even keep running the ones we already have. We would not be able to continue living in the way that we have gotten used to.

Conservationists know that our supplies of some non-renewable resources cannot last much longer at the rate we are now using them. If we want to have those resources in the future, we will have to learn how to stretch the supplies we still have.

The next chapters will tell some ways we can do that.

Five

Save It! Keep It! Use It Again!

One easy way of using up our resources more slowly is just to use less of them.

We can save heating oil by keeping our homes and offices and schools a little cooler in the winter.

We can save gasoline by driving smaller cars, and by not driving when we don't have to. When we save heating oil and gasoline, we are saving the petroleum from which they are made.

We can save electricity by turning out lights and turning off machines that we aren't really using. Coal and petroleum are used to make much of our electricity, so we can be saving those resources when we turn off an electrical device.

Having fewer things is another way that we can slow down our use of resources. Some people may not like that idea. But sooner or later we are probably going to have to get used to it.

Many people already know that they don't really need all the toys, clothes, and television sets they have. And some of them know that if we can make do with a little less right now, we can

be more sure of having enough in times to come.

We could stretch our resources quite a bit just by keeping things longer. People often throw away clothing, dishes, and even furniture and cars just because they get tired of them, or because styles change. A lot of our resources get used up in replacing perfectly good things that people have tossed into the trash.

Do you think that's the way it has to be?

Many things that people throw away are torn or broken. But often those things can be mended so that they are good as new, or nearly so. Many an old bicycle, chair, or bookcase has been fixed up and painted to look like a new one.

Is there something around your home you could do that with?

Sometimes you might not be able to use
something any longer, even though it's still good.
You might have outgrown a bicycle or a sweater.

Instead of throwing those things away, you could
pass them on to a younger brother or sister, or
someone else who could use them. Maybe you
could get another bike or sweater from someone a
little older than you who has outgrown one.

You might call things like that "hand-me-downs." But there is another way to talk about things that are being used again. We can say that they have been *recycled*.

If you use an old paint bucket to collect earthworms for going fishing, then you could say that you have recycled the bucket. String that you save from a package is recycled when you use it to bundle some newspapers.

When you recycle something, it can mean that someone else is using it for the same purpose that you used it for. Or it can mean that you are using it again for the same purpose or for a different purpose than you first used it for.

Using less stuff such as fuel, having fewer things and keeping them longer, fixing up old things instead of getting new ones, recycling whatever you can—all are good ways to make our natural resources go further.

And whenever we keep something or give it to someone else instead of throwing it away, we are also cutting down on the amount of trash that we will have. Trash is not so easy to get rid of as you might think—so the less there is of it, the better.

We will talk more about trash later on in this book.

Six

One More Time

Some things can be recycled just as they are. A returnable soft-drink bottle—the kind you pay a deposit on—is a good example.

You return the bottle to the store to get your deposit back. Then the bottle goes back to the bottling company, where it is sterilized and refilled with soda pop. The same bottle can make many trips back and forth that way.

But many soft drinks come in "no deposit—no return" bottles. Those bottles are not strong enough to be used again. Still, they need not be tossed into the trash basket. The glass they are made of can be recycled, even if the bottles themselves cannot.

Your town may have a recycling center where

bottles are collected. It might be called a recycling station or depot.

The bottles are usually smashed up at the recycling center, to make them take up less space. Then they go to a bottle factory, where the glass is ground up and melted down to make new bottles.

Aluminum can be recycled in much the same way as glass. Soft-drink cans made of aluminum are always welcome at a recycling center. You can tell an aluminum can from other kinds because it has a rounded bottom and will *not* stick to a magnet.

The aluminum cans are crushed at the recycling center, and then sent to a factory where they are melted down to make new cans of the same kind.

If you have a choice, it is better to buy soft drinks in returnable bottles than in non-returnable bottles or cans. Some glass or aluminum is always wasted in making new bottles or cans, and it also takes more energy (and more fuel) to make a new bottle or can than to sterilize a used bottle. Besides, soft drinks are cheaper in returnable bottles.

If you can't get returnable bottles where you live, then the next best thing is to take your non-returnable bottles or cans to your town's recycling center. While you are at it, take along your old newspapers. They can be recycled, too.

Not that we can use the very same newspaper over again on another day. But the newsprint—the paper on which a newspaper is printed—can be ground up, cleaned of ink, and made into new paper for printing another day's news.

Many different kinds of raw materials can be recycled, if we want to take the trouble to do it.

Have you ever seen a place where old autos are junked? It is almost like a mine of iron, copper, aluminum, and many other metals. People are finding new ways of recycling the raw materials found in old cars and refrigerators and such.

As we begin to run out of some metals, or as they become more expensive to dig out of the earth, we will turn more toward mining our junk yards and trash baskets for the materials we need.

That will mean less trash to pile up, and less litter, too. A recycled can or bottle is one that will not be left in a park, at the beach, or along the highway.

Seven

Instant Trash

If you were to browse through your family's trash bin some afternoon, you would probably find that most of the trash is made up of packages of one kind or another, or parts of packages.

Cardboard boxes, paper wrappings, paper and plastic bags, cellophane and string, not to mention cans, bottles, and jars.

Some of the packaging is needed, such as a bottle to hold orange juice or a jar to hold pickles, and a label to tell what's inside.

But much of the packaging we are used to is not needed.

Look around in a hardware store and see how things are packaged there. You will find many small items such as electrical plugs and cabinet hinges in cardboard packages covered with a plastic bubble. Usually the package is much larger than the thing that is being sold. And often the thing inside does not really need a package at all.

The same is true for a lot of small things you will find in a toy store or a dime store. Often you could carry them home in your pocket, if it weren't for the big packages they are in.

The bubble pack usually has no use once you've taken the thing you bought out of it. It can only be thrown away. You could call it instant trash.

All of that cardboard and plastic being tossed out wastes the trees that are used to make the cardboard, and the petroleum that is used to make the plastic. It also wastes the energy that was used to make the cardboard and plastic from those raw materials. And it leaves us with a lot of extra rubbish.

Do you think we should do anything about that kind of packaging?

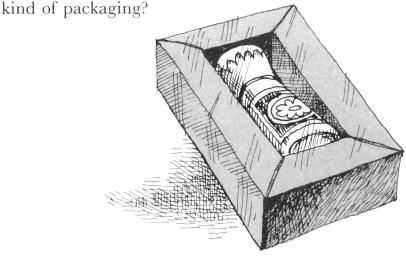

Some hamburger stands will serve you a
hamburger wrapped in paper and tucked inside a
cardboard box. Then they will put the box inside
a bag—even though you are carrying the
hamburger to a table only a few feet away.

Is all that wrapping, boxing, and bagging really
needed for a hamburger?

A man's shirt comes back from a laundry with a piece of cardboard inside it, and a plastic clip on the collar. The shirt is inside a plastic bag, and there is a paper wrapper around that.

Can you see how that sort of packaging wastes our natural resources?

You can help to save our resources by not using more packaging than you need to, when you have a choice.

Suppose you were buying just a loaf of bread at a grocery store. It is probably already wrapped in paper, and there may even be a plastic bag around that. You certainly don't need a paper bag to carry it home in.

You can ask the clerk in a store not to give you a bag when you are buying something small enough to fit in your pocket. Some people carry their own sack or basket to the store, so that they will not need a paper bag even when they are buying several things.

We use up a lot of our natural resources making things that we really need. Do you think there is any sense in using up more of our resources to make packages that we don't need at all?

Eight

Use It Once and Throw It Away?

In our country today we have a great many things that are meant to be used just once, and then thrown away. For some things, that is not a bad idea—tissues and toilet paper, for example. Or the flat wooden sticks that the doctor uses to hold down your tongue while you say "Ahh." It would be more trouble than it was worth to clean those things. And they could spread germs if they weren't cleaned well enough.

But the "use it once and throw it away" idea may not be such a good one when it comes to some other things.

For a long time we had paper plates and cups and thin wooden forks and spoons for picnicking. They could not be cleaned easily. We threw them away when the picnic was over.

Now we have plastic dishes and cups and plastic knives and forks and spoons. We are told that these, too, are disposable—meant to be thrown away. But that is a lot of plastic to be tossing out.

We don't want to take our good dishes or silverware along on a picnic. Those things are heavy, and they could get lost or broken. But we can use plastic dishes and cups and forks instead, and wash them off when we have finished eating.

We don't have to throw plastic picnic things away just because someone says they are disposable. If we want to, we can use them over and over again. That saves our petroleum resources, and it saves us money, too.

Bread, fruit, shirts, and sweaters come packed in plastic bags. Many people throw those bags away. Then they buy new plastic bags to put leftovers and sandwiches and other things in. Does that make much sense?

Think about the paper bags that groceries are put in at the store. Most people throw those bags away when they get home, even though the bags are still good. If you don't have a way to use those bags, see whether the store will take them back. Some stores might not; but other stores will be glad to have them.

We used to think about tissues and napkins and such when we talked of disposable items. But now we have disposable diapers for babies, and disposable dresses and underpants for women. They are supposed to be thrown away after they have been worn only once.

There are flashlights that we are to toss into the waste basket when they go dead, instead of putting in a new bulb or battery.

Some people find all of these disposable things convenient to use. But that is an awful lot of good paper, plastic, glass, and metal to be putting into the trash.

When we toss aside a plastic bag or cup, or a "disposable" flashlight, we are taking our non-renewable natural resources and simply throwing them away. Now that we are beginning to run short of some of those resources, maybe it is time to start thinking twice about what we are doing.

"Waste not, want not," said our ancestors. What do you suppose they meant by that?

Nine

Where to Stash the Trash?

Today we produce lots of TV sets, station wagons, washing machines, baseball gloves, toy soldiers, and countless other things. But one of the main things we produce is trash.

Think of all the worn-out light bulbs and toasters ... the outgrown clothing and broken toys ... yesterday's newspaper or last week's magazine ... "one-way" soda bottles and cans ... cardboard boxes and plastic bubble packs ... paper bags and disposable dishes.

When the garbage truck pulls up and takes away our rubbish, we think that is the end of it. But it is really just the beginning. The trash that gets picked up at our door will have to be put down someplace. Where?

Many towns just dump their trash in a huge heap outside of town and try to forget about it. But a town dump is an ugly, smelly place. Rats come to feed on the garbage. Fires get started in the trash and pour black smoke into the air.

In some places, great pits are dug to toss the trash into. Each day some of the earth that was dug up is used to cover the trash. That helps keep the stuff from smelling too bad, and helps keep rats and flies away. A dump of this kind, called a landfill, is better than an open dump.

But in time a landfill gets filled. Then the town has to find a new place to dump its trash.

In the past, swamps and marshes have often been used as landfill areas. But now we know that dumping trash in a swamp or marsh kills animals and plants that may live there and nowhere else. Conservationists don't want to lose those plants and animals. So other places must be found for the town's rubbish.

One idea that has been tried is to keep on adding trash and earth to a landfill, even after it has been filled up. That makes a hill or even a small mountain. Some cities have used such hills for skiing in the winter.

But we cannot really use very many garbage mountains. We still have to find other ways of getting rid of our trash, or at least making it take up less space.

Machines called compactors can squeeze and squash our trash so that much more of it will fit in a landfill. Many towns now compact their trash before dumping it.

In some places, special compactors have been used to squeeze trash into very hard blocks that can be used for building. The garbage building blocks are covered with plastic so they won't smell.

Burning is another way of making garbage take up less space. And the heat from burning garbage can be used to run a power plant that produces electricity. That helps get rid of our garbage and gives us some useful energy, too.

But it is very difficult to burn garbage without making a lot of smoke to dirty the air. And there are still a lot of cinders and ashes to get rid of. And lots of stuff made of metal and glass that doesn't get burned up at all.

Right now there really isn't any very good way of getting rid of our garbage. But the ways we do have would work better if we just had less of it.

One of our biggest problems right now is that we are running short of some of our needed resources, or that they are becoming very expensive to take from the earth. Another big problem is that we have many times more trash than we know what to do with.

Much of that trash is made up of the very resources that we need for making new things.

Do you see how conservation and recycling of our natural resources can help to solve both problems at once?

Index

DATE DUE